SHARPiE® ART WORKSHOP FOR KiDS

Fun, Easy, and Creative Drawing and Crafts Projects ▪ KATHY BARBRO

ROCKPORT

Quarto is the authority on a wide range of topics.

Quarto educates, entertains and enriches the lives of our readers—enthusiasts and lovers of hands-on living.

www.QuartoKnows.com

First published in the United States of America in 2016 by
Rockport Publishers, an Imprint of
Quarto Publishing Group USA Inc.
100 Cummings Center
Suite 406-L
Beverly, Massachusetts 01915-6101
Telephone: (978) 282-9590
Fax: (978) 283-2742
QuartoKnows.com
Visit our blogs at QuartoKnows.com

10 9 8 7 6 5 4 3 2

ISBN: 978-1-63159-251-5

Library of Congress Cataloging-in-Publication Data
Barbro, Kathy, author.
Sharpie art workshop for kids : fun, easy, and creative drawing and
crafts projects / Kathy Barbro.
ISBN 978-1-63159-251-5 (paperback)
1. Felt marker decoration. 2. Felt marker drawing--Technique.
TT386 .B37 2016
745.5--dc23
2016025768

Design: Laura McFadden
Photography: Kathy Barbro, except by Glenn Scott Photography on front cover
All artwork by Kathy Barbro unless otherwise noted

Printed in China

*This book is dedicated with love to my parents, Carl and Ruth.
Growing up on a little farm in Indiana meant learning how to climb trees,
bake cookies, shell corn, and much more. Those experiences were the
foundation to a grown-up life that finds joy in creativity, no matter where
I live, or how old I might get. And for that, I am forever grateful.*

CONTENTS

Page 68

Page 84

PREFACE

Children's art comes with its own natural charm, but the tools that kids use can either minimize or maximize it. Give a young boy or girl some average crayons and paper and you'll probably get a nice enough picture. But give them some supplies that make bold, vivid color and a lesson that sparks creativity, and amazing things can happen. My passion over the past fifteen years has been to find and create art projects that bring these elements together, and more often than not, they use one of my most relied upon supplies—Sharpie markers. Thick or thin, black or color, metallic or poster, they enhance whatever material they go on, and seem to highlight the originality of any child who uses them. I'm excited to share these brand-new marker projects from myself and a few other passionate art teachers and bloggers, who have come to view Sharpie markers as a staple in our homes and classrooms.

Cat drawing by Zach G., 1st grade

A Note to Kids

You are so lucky to be living in a time when there's a steady stream of new art tools to try out. I have sometimes told my students, "When I was your age, the most exciting thing I could get was a 64 set box of crayons . . . and I liked it!" Today, supplies come in a huge assortment of colors—many with added glitter, sparkle, and shine—you don't even have to go out of your way to find them. Most, like Sharpie markers, can be found at arts, crafts, and even office supply stores. My wish for you is to try out as many as you can to see what they can do. You never know where inspiration might come from, but playing and experimenting is a good place to start.

A Note to Parents

Consider your good fortune to have so many art materials to try out with your kids. There are more options and varieties than ever before. You can now color or dye or weave or paint or hot glue together all kinds of things that I could only have dreamed of as a kid. What that means for you, parents, is that there truly is an art activity for every child to connect to, something he or she will not only like, but will possibly excel at. Finding joy in art can lead to a future career, or just as important, a hobby that brings a sense of personal satisfaction. Your kids can't lose; they just need to get started.

Hey, Kids!

WELCOME TO THE WORKSHOP

MAKE YOUR MARK

Every Sharpie marker is designed to do at least one job really well, and most can do many more. These are the ones I use most frequently for kids' projects, both at home and at school.

Sharpie Fine Point

A classic black fine point is the Sharpie marker I use for outlining, in both drawings and watercolor paintings.

The colors in the fine point tip width are beautifully vibrant, especially on glossy finger paint paper. They can be used for many different crafts projects and are a good alternative to paints for very young students.

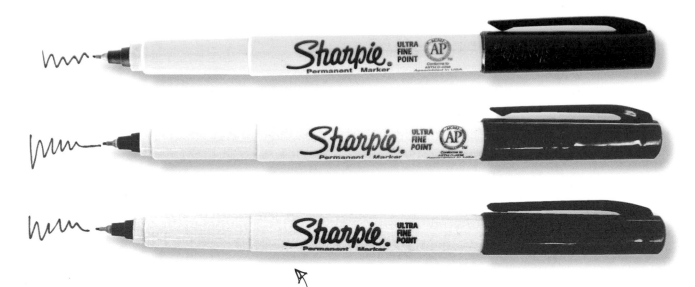

Sharpie Ultra-Fine Point

Both the black and the colors in this tip width are great for drawing fine details. They also work well for adding visual texture to softer surfaces, such as aluminum foil.

Sharpie Chisel Tip

Use these when bold lines are needed for large drawings and areas need to be colored really black, as with silhouettes.

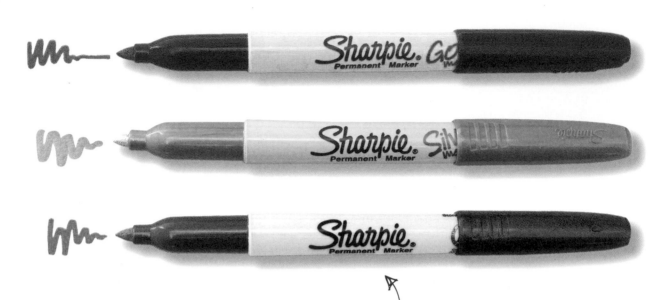

Gold, Silver, and Bronze Fine Point

These metallic colors look best on dark paper, especially black. They're also great for adding metallic highlights to paintings and drawings.

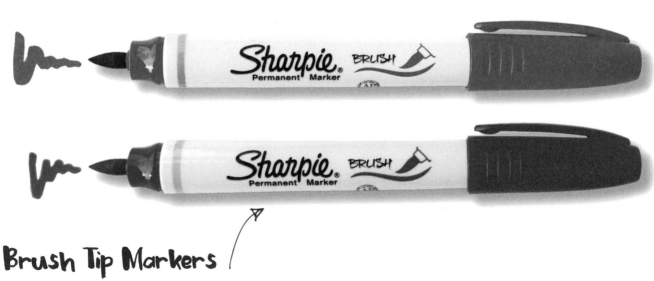

Brush Tip Markers

The soft yet sturdy brush tips help students fill color in a way that can't be matched. They work well on paper, foil, wood, glass, ceramics, and canvas, just to name a few types of surfaces.

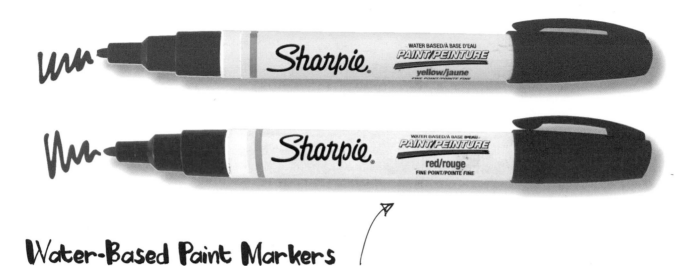

Water-Based Paint Markers

These markers are great for opaque color on paper and craft projects that won't get a lot of wear and tear.

Oil-Based Paint Markers

These are a special treat for kids when an opaque color is needed for plastic or glass craft projects. The oil base also makes them shiny and more durable than the water-based versions.

THE WELL-STOCKED ART ROOM

Whether at home or at school, these are the art supplies I reach for time and time again. Some need to be purchased, but you can find many others around the house or through recycling.

Papers and Other Art Surfaces

- Acetate (or overhead projector sheets)
- Aluminum foil
- Cardstock paper from the crafts store (all colors, especially black)
- Coffee filters, white round type (flattened with a steam iron)
- Dry wax paper (may be found at restaurant supply stores or online; see page 26 for more information)
- Finger paint paper
- Multimedia paper
- Tissue paper (bleeding, madras pattern, and craft variety)
- Watercolor paper

Paints

- Acrylic craft paint
- Cake or pan tempera paint
- Liquid watercolor paint

Drawing Tools

- Color sticks
- Crayons
- Permanent markers

Crafts Materials

- Craft glue
- Duct tape
- Foam letters
- Glue sticks
- Googly eyes
- Mini cupcake liners
- Metal tape (from a hardware store)
- Popsicle sticks
- Pom-poms
- White glue

Household and Recycled Items

- Bread ties
- Cardboard
- CD tray containers
- Chipboard
- Dried beans
- Dry pasta
- Old CDs
- Old rubber gloves
- Pizza boxes
- Tin cans
- Wine corks

Here's a great first project: Show the world how creative you are by making your own hand-colored pencils.

THE ELEMENTS OF ART

The elements of art are the visual building blocks artists use to create their work. The better you understand these elements and the role each plays in making art, the more your art-making skills will improve.

I created these visual examples to illustrate and give meaning to each one of them.

Line

A *line* is a mark that has width, direction, and length.

Shape

A *shape* is a closed line that's two-dimensional, flat, and limited in height and width.

Color

Color, which is produced when light is reflected from a surface to the eye, has three main characteristics: hue, value, and intensity. (See pages 18 and 19 for more information on color.)

Space

Artists use the element of *space* to create a feeling of depth or dimension.

Form

The element of *form* gives a subject depth, as well as width and height, and is also used to teach about perspective.

Value

Value is the relative lightness or darkness of a color. High-value or light colors are used to represent highlights, while low-value or dark colors are used to represent shadows.

Texture

In art, *texture* refers to the way things feel, or look as if they might feel if touched.

COLOR BASICS

Learning more about colors and the words to describe them will help you choose the best colors for your art. Here are some of the main categories, along with an example of each.

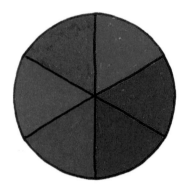  

The Color Wheel

A color wheel organizes colors around a circle to show how they relate to each other. This example shows primary and secondary colors.

Primary Colors

The primaries—red, yellow, and blue—are the three colors you need to mix secondary colors. They're bright and bold, and sure to catch your attention.

Secondary Colors

The secondaries—orange, green, and purple—are made when two primary colors are mixed together. Secondary colors can give you a deeper, richer color palette.

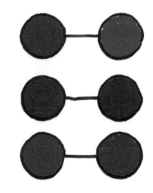

Warm and Cool Colors

The color wheel can also be split into two groups to create different feelings. Red, orange, and yellow are warm, while purple, blue, and green are cool. If you want your art to have a cozy glow, then lots of warm colors would be good. Or if it's a chilly look you're going for, then reach for the cool. Do you want to make your art really pop off the background? Try using one group within another.

Complementary Colors

These colors are located across from each other on the color wheel. When placed side by side, they make each other look brighter than if viewed on their own.

Analogous Colors

Analogous colors are next to each other on the color wheel; for example, orange and red or green and blue. They're a good choice when you want to blend colors, because when they overlap, they make a nice, gradual change into each other.

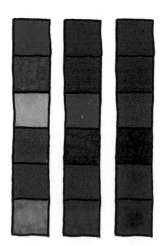

Tinting and Shading

To tint a color, you need to add white; to shade it, you add black. Doing so will help you create highlights and shadows in your artwork.

DRAWING TiPS

After years of drawing with children, I've noticed that many beginners share several tendencies. While there is no substitute for practice, I find that these tips make things a little less frustrating.

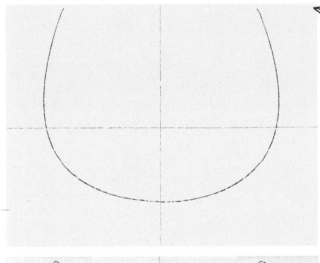

Whenever possible, use light pencil lines as guides across the middle of the paper to help you plan and center your artwork.

Look for simple, symmetrical projects like this cat head. Extra curvy and unsymmetrical drawings seem to be more difficult for most. Start with the biggest shape first, and watch the center line so the shape is symmetrical and balanced.

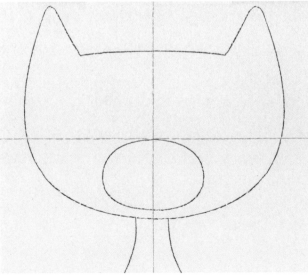

After your big shapes are done, start to fill in with the smaller ones. Keep in mind that most children tend to draw on the small side, so check your shapes often to make sure they're the right size.

Trace pencil lines with a marker so they'll show up really well. Erase any remaining pencil lines to keep your art neat and looking its best.

Always color in shapes carefully. Using the sides of markers and crayons will help make solid colors, without any scribbles showing.

TRACING AWAY

Over the years, my students have taught me a new appreciation for the simple joy of tracing pictures. As a free-time option in my classroom, many happily search out a drawing book, place a piece of tissue paper over a page, and zone out as they carefully trace each line as accurately as possible. This exercise will never replace skills learned from observational drawing, but it seems to make a connection for those who don't feel particularly skilled in that area. And at the very least, it's pretty good practice for fine motor skills too.

Here are my suggestions for stocking a tracing station at home or in school.

Buy a box of sandwich wrap for your "see-through" paper. It's much less expensive than tissue paper, so you don't have to worry too much about waste.

Keep a stash of drawing books on hand. They usually have lots of line art that's easy to trace.

Visit ClipArt ETC (see page 126) for free drawings to print out. They proudly support schools by providing thousands of free downloadable black-and-white illustrations. You can find cool line drawings of alphabets, animals, plants, historical landmarks, and much more.

Scribble, scrabble.

ALL ABOUT ART

Color inside and outside of the lines. Go ahead, get messy and have fun!

Sharpie
Permanent Marker BRUSH

SCRIBBLE-SCRABBLE HEARTS

This heart collage on canvas benefits from a free-form style of coloring. Try using and layering at least four colors in each box so your canvas has a rich collection of marker color.

Project Checklist

- Stretched canvas
- Pencil
- Assorted brush tip and fine point Sharpie markers
- Dry wax paper
  (see note below)
- White glue
- Water-based sealer
  (such as Mod Podge aerosol pray)
- Copy paper
- Utility scissors

What's Dry Wax Paper?

Dry wax paper is a lot like regular wax paper, but much thinner. It is often used for serving fast food, such as pizza, so you can find it at most restaurant supply stores. If not, go online. Just be sure to search for *dry* wax paper, as the regular kitchen variety won't work—it doesn't "hug" the canvas after it's dry the way dry wax paper does.

1. Divide canvas into desired grid with light pencil lines. This sample is 16" x 20" (40.6 x 50.8 cm) and divided into 3" x 4" (7.6 x 10.1 cm) boxes.

2. Draw a black box on copy paper and use as a template to trace and color hearts on dry wax paper. Color with markers, layering and blending as you go.

3. Continue making hearts until you have enough to fill the canvas. Try to have a large variety of colors both inside and outside each heart.

4. Trim each heart box, very close to the edge, and arrange on the canvas. Make sure to spread out any similar colors so the backgrounds are always different.

5. Mix white glue with water in a 50/50 ratio. Working with one box and heart at a time, brush the mixture onto both the canvas *and* the back of each heart. Place the heart on the canvas and brush more mixture on top so the paper is totally saturated. Smooth continually to eliminate any bubbles.

6. Work in rows until the canvas is filled. Check for bubbles again when complete. When the dry wax paper dries, it will cling and look like it is part of the canvas. For a shiny finish, cover with a glossy sealer after the dry wax paper is dry.

ART SCHOOL 101: Try this as a class project. Have each student color or draw a self-portrait in his or her own box. It works great for fundraisers where a more finished piece of art is called for.

ETCHED FOIL FISH

This giant fish is made with a few ordinary
supplies, but its foil color and etched texture
make it look pretty special when complete.

Project Checklist

- Corrugated cardboard
- Glue stick
- Aluminum foil
- Utility scissors
- Assorted brush tip and
  ultra-fine point Sharpie
  markers

ART SCHOOL 101: This project uses several elements of art: lines, color, and texture. Before children are
finished, ask them to consider if they've used all of them in the most complete way possible. This foil fish looks
great with lots of layered color and then marker texture on top, but children need to be encouraged to work that
thoroughly.

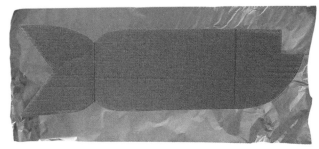

1. Cut a large simple fish shape from an old piece of cardboard. (See below for ideas of other fish shapes.) My sample is about 25" (63 cm) long. If there are folds in the cardboard, you can make them fall on the neck or tail lines.

2. Cover one side generously with a glue stick. Make sure the glue is thick enough that you can see it, especially in folds and creases. The project will succeed only if all of the foil is completely adhered to the cardboard.

3. Use utility scissors to trim all around the fish, cutting through the foil *and* cardboard, very close to the edge. The pressure from cutting will seal the edges together.

4. Divide the fish into sections (head, body, and tail) with a black marker and fill in all with a background color. Layer large bands of color and stripes on top. Use an ultra-fine point marker to draw scales and texture. When complete, trace the outside edge of the fish with a black marker.

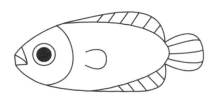
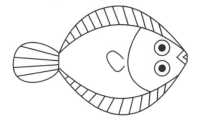
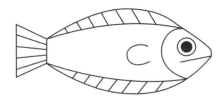

Some other fish shapes to try!

MINI ABSTRACT PORTRAIT

Sharpie brush tip markers can be mixed together on most surfaces, just like paint. Your kids can blend and create what looks like an oil painting, with all of the vivid color and none of the mess.

This project shows how the simplest shapes can be arranged to create an image, and how color and value can be used to create dimension and depth.

Project Checklist

- Mini canvas and easel (found at craft chain stores and online)
- Pencil
- Sharpie brush tip markers in assorted colors (we used berry, black, blue, green, orange, purple, red, and yellow)
- Water-based sealer (such as Mod Podge aerosol spray)

1. Lightly sketch a symmetrical face on the canvas with a pencil.

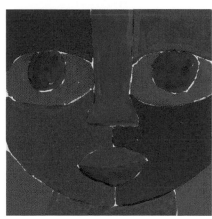

2. Color in the face, using a different marker for each area so there's contrast between the areas that are right next to each other.

3. Add a squiggle of a darker color or value within each area as shown: along the left side of the nose; in the areas above the eyes and along the nose; within each of the eyes, along their top edges; on the outer edges of the cheeks; on the left side of the neck; and in the areas on either side of the neck.

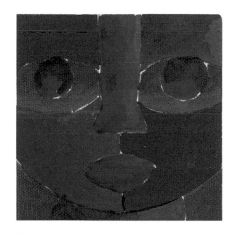

4. Use the color or value you used in Step 2 to blend in the color you applied in Step 3, leaving some of the original color visible.

5. Outline each shape in black. Apply a sealer to give the portrait a glossy finish. Let dry.

ART SCHOOL 101: This project works best when analogous colors are used in Step 3 to add depth to each of the base colors—red over orange, purple over blue, orange over yellow.

WARM AND COOL ECHO FLOWERS

Project by Cheryl Trowbridge, owner of Teach Kids Art website

Creating "echo lines" is great practice for young artists. Cheryl Trowbridge, who helps adults share the joy of art with kids, shows how to use this technique to make beautiful art with warm or cool color patterns.

Project Checklist

- Pencil
- Drawing paper
- Black fine point Sharpie marker
- Cool and warm colored markers

1. Draw a simple flower in the center of your paper. Be sure to include a stem and some leaves.

2. Draw parallel lines that "echo" the shape of your flower, spacing them about the width of a pencil apart. Continue until they touch every edge of your paper.

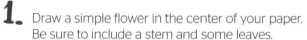

3. Choose a color scheme for your drawing. You could choose warm colors (red, yellow, orange) as shown here, or cool colors (blue, green, purple), as shown opposite. Be sure to color neatly and fill in all the white areas.

PiCASSO TiSSUE PAPER PORTRAIT

Project by Mary Beggs Bosley, owner of MaryMaking blog

Mary Bosley combined her fine arts and graphic design backgrounds to create this simple abstract line drawing in the Cubist style of Pablo Picasso. Some added bits of random color can be a truly beautiful thing.

Project Checklist

- Watercolor paper
- Pencil
- Black fine point Sharpie marker
- Paintbrush
- Water
- Bleeding tissue paper
- Utility scissors *(optional)*
- Heavy books

1. 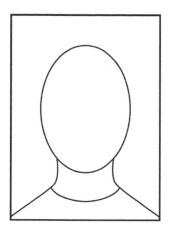 Using a pencil, draw an oval head. Add a neck and shoulders below.

2. 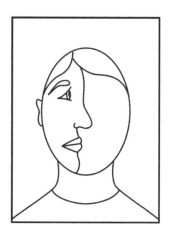 On the left, draw a profile face with profile features. Add a hairline.

3.  Finish the right side of the face with a forward-looking eye. Add hair and trace all of the lines with a Sharpie marker.

4. 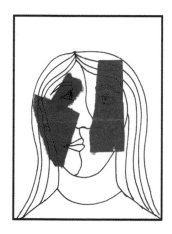 Brush the drawing with water. Tear or cut pieces of tissue paper and apply as shown until the face is covered.

5. 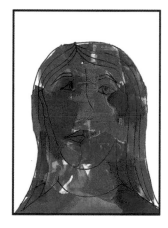 Let dry. Remove the tissue paper and press under heavy books to flatten any curled edges.

ART SCHOOL 101: Cubism is an early twentieth-century art movement that is often credited to Pablo Picasso. It experimented with displaying several aspects of the same object at the same time. This portrait is a great way for children to learn about Cubism. For a variation, have kids draw Picasso's *Dove of Peace* and then color in the same manner.

TOOLED METAL BUG

Project by Nic Hahn, owner of Mini Matisse blog

Here's a project from art teacher Nic Hahn that gives you the chance to work in three dimensions with some fun materials like metal tooling and pipe cleaners. And who wouldn't want to create their very own bug with supplies like these?

Project Checklist

- Bug tracing template
  (*see page 109*)
- Paper
- Colored pencil
- Tape
- Metal tooling foil
- Felt
- Pencil
- Utility scissors
- Assorted fine point
  Sharpie markers
- Chenille sticks (pipe
  cleaners) and/or
  colorful wire
- Hot glue gun
- Tag board

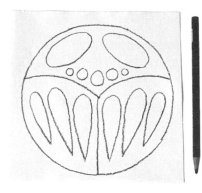

1. Trace the body of your bug on a sheet of paper with a colored pencil.

2. Tape the design onto the metal tooling.

3. Place the metal tooling on top of the felt. Trace with a dull pencil over all the lines on your design. The design will start pressing through onto the metal.

4. After taking the paper off the metal, cut the shape of your bug body out of the metal.

5. First, test out the colors on the scrap metal. Then use Sharpie markers to color the side of the bug with the raised areas.

6. Create the legs, wings, and/or antenna with the chenille sticks or colorful wire. Hot glue the legs and metal bug onto a tag board for display.

O'KEEFFE RELIEF FLOWERS

This textured and colorful art uses Georgia O'Keeffe's idea of filling an entire canvas with one beautiful flower.

Project Checklist

- Chipboard
- Pencil
- White glue
- Glue stick
- Aluminum foil
- Brush tip Sharpie markers in assorted colors
- Fine point Sharpie marker

ART SCHOOL 101: Georgia O'Keeffe was a pioneer of modern art and created large-scale paintings of natural forms and flowers at close range. Young artists tend to draw small, so imitating her style of drawing off the page will help them see how great their art can look when it's really *big*.

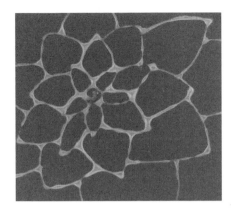

1. Draw a flower in pencil on a piece of chipboard. Trace with white glue and let dry.

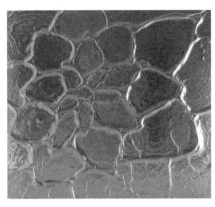

2. Cover the chipboard generously with a glue stick. Tear a sheet of foil and apply, shiny side up. Rub the foil thoroughly with fingers. Wrap the extra foil around the edges and glue in place.

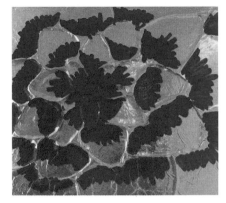

3. Use a marker to color the base of each petal with a chosen main color. This sample is colored with a red marker.

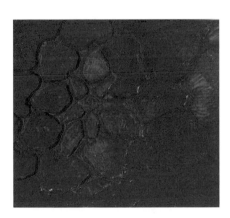

4. Color the rest of each petal with a similar, analogous color, such as orange. Use a fine point marker to add lines inside each petal (shown opposite).

Variations

Another fun marker combination is blue and violet, which create a purple when overlapped. Pink and yellow are good for a lighter look and create orange when they touch.

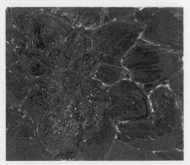

Draw an O'Keeffe Flower

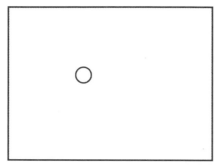

1. Draw a small circle.

2. Draw five petals around the circle.

3. Draw five larger petals in between the smaller ones.

4. Repeat with five even larger petals.

5. Repeat with another five petals. It's okay if they go off the page.

6. Add any petal lines to break up the background.

BRIGHTS ON BLACK

Children love to add patterns to their drawings. Outlining them with a metallic marker adds even more fun to the process.

Project Checklist

- Watercolor paper
- Pencil
- Black fine point Sharpie marker
- Liquid watercolor paint
- Silver Sharpie marker

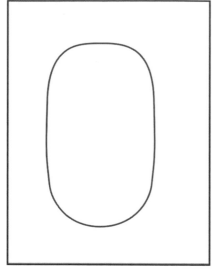

1. Draw an oval for the body in pencil.

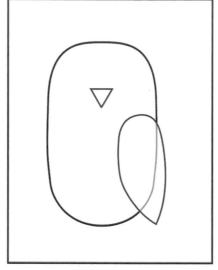

2. Add beak and wing. Erase the line inside.

3. Draw outer eye lines as shown.

4. Draw inside eyes.

5. Add chest and head lines.

6. Draw zigzag lines across chest.

7. Draw branch, feet, and wing circles.

8. Add tail and leaves.

ART SCHOOL 101:
Watercolor pan paints or paint tablets have their place in the art room for mixing colors and other uses, but I've found that young artists often do much better starting with liquid watercolors. By having the paint ready to go in cups, and not needing to first brush water on tablets, they can just concentrate on controlling the color, which is a skill in itself. Many online art stores offer their own line of liquid watercolor paints.

9. Add more branches and leaves, then add the moon.

10. Trace and paint the owl with warm colors and the back with black. Finish by adding silver marker lines just outside all the black lines. Add stars to the sky.

LINE ART LEAVES

Thin parallel lines create art with a delicate, transparent quality.

Project Checklist

- White cardstock paper, 5" x 7.5" (12.7 x 19 cm)
- Pencil
- Ultra-fine point Sharpie markers in assorted colors
- Glue stick
- Colored cardstock paper, 8.5" x 11" (21.6 x 28 cm)

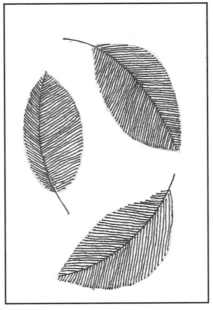

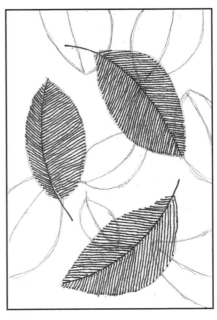

1. Sketch three leaves lightly with a pencil.

2. Trace the spine and fill each leaf with lines very close to each other.

3. Draw more leaves that fill in spaces and overlap just a small amount.

4. Fill in leaves with lines as before.

5. Add more leaves to balance the composition, and fill with lines. Erase all the pencil lines and frame with a sheet of cardstock.

ART SCHOOL 101:
This project can illustrate the beauty of line art. For the best results, make sure your starting pencil lines are drawn very lightly so they can be erased. Try to keep the overlapping to small sections. If not, the parallel lines can get a little confusing.

SHIMMERING SEA LIFE

Project by Gail Bartel, owner of That Artist Woman blog

Art supplies can sometimes be found in unusual places, like a hardware store. Art educator Gail Bartel created this project using metal tape. The fish look great colored with marker and will always lie nice and flat, thanks to the adhesive backing.

Project Checklist

- Watercolor paper, trimmed to 8" x 11" (20.3 x 27.9 cm)
- White crayon
- Blue liquid watercolor paint
- Metal tape, cut into 4" to 5" (10.2 to 12.7 cm) pieces
- Black fine point Sharpie marker
- Fine point Sharpie markers in assorted colors
- Utility scissors
- Glue stick
- Black paper, 9" x 12" (22.9 x 30.5 cm)

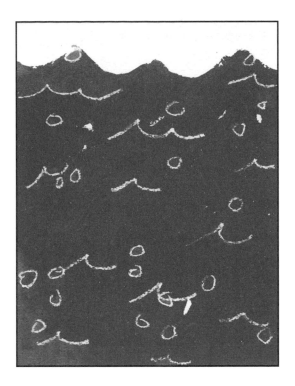

1. Draw waves and bubbles with a white crayon on the watercolor paper. Paint with blue water-color paint to reveal the white lines.

2. Draw fish on the metal tape with a black Sharpie marker. Try to make some from different points of view. Lay them on the watercolor paper until they seem to fill the page. Color them in with markers and trim out with scissors.

3. Peel off the back of the tape and apply to the watercolor paper. Give your artwork a frame by gluing it to a larger piece of black paper.

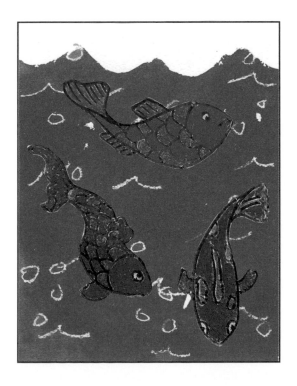

FOLK ART LANDSCAPE

Project by Laura Lohmann, owner of Painted Paper Art blog

Folk art is the art of the everyday, rooted in traditions that come from a community. Laura Lohmann, an elementary school art teacher from Ohio, explores this art form by creating a country landscape with patterned fields.

Project Checklist

- White drawing paper
- Pencil
- Black fine point Sharpie marker
- Oil pastels or crayons
- Liquid watercolor paints in assorted colors
- Glue stick
- Large colored paper for matting
- Scrap painted paper

1. Using a pencil, draw a landscape with lots of space for fields. Divide the space into about fifteen different sections. Add various patterns and designs to the shapes representing different crops. Using a black Sharpie marker, trace over all the lines, from the shapes to all the different patterns.

2. Using oil pastels or crayons, color in some of the smaller shapes and patterns.

3. Paint the background with liquid watercolor paints. Let dry. Mat onto larger paper and frame with strips of colored paper to create a border around the painting.

Let's get exotic!

AROUND THE
WORLD

Visit wild places through your
awesome Sharpie marker drawings.

AFRICAN MASK DRAWINGS

These masks are drawn and then traced onto madras tissue paper with the thickest of the Sharpie markers. The bold, black lines on the colorful paper make a very vivid image.

Project Checklist

- Drawing template *(see page 111)*
- Cardstock paper
- Pencil
- Glue stick
- Madras tissue paper
- Black chisel tip Sharpie marker
- Black fine point Sharpie marker

ART SCHOOL 101: Many children learn about different cultures at school, so this is a way to integrate art with social studies. It's also fun to dabble in symbolic drawing and not worry about making anything look realistic.

1. Fold cardstock paper in half. Draw the mask features on one side, with the fold in the center. Unfold and draw the other side of the mask to match as closely as possible.

2. Rub the glue stick all over the drawing. Center a large sheet of tissue on top. Smooth with fingers.

3. Turn the paper over and wrap the tissue around the edges. Glue in place.

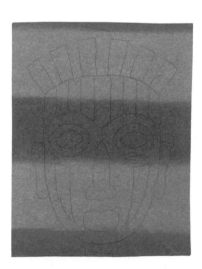

4. Turn the art over; pencil lines will show through the tissue.

5. Trace all lines with the large chisel tip marker to make them bold. Fill in some shapes black and then add lines and dots with the fine point marker.

Variation

Here's another mask design to try. See the drawing template on page 111.

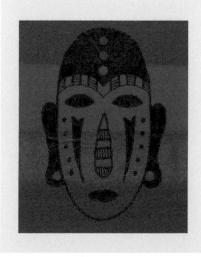

SPARKLING ABORIGINAL JELLYFISH

Two of my favorite types of markers, metallic and paint, just happen to look best on black paper. Here you can make some delicate-looking jellyfish using a dot technique favored by ancient Australian artists.

Project Checklist

- Black cardstock paper
- Pencil
- Metallic Sharpie markers in gold and bronze
- White water-based medium tip Sharpie paint marker

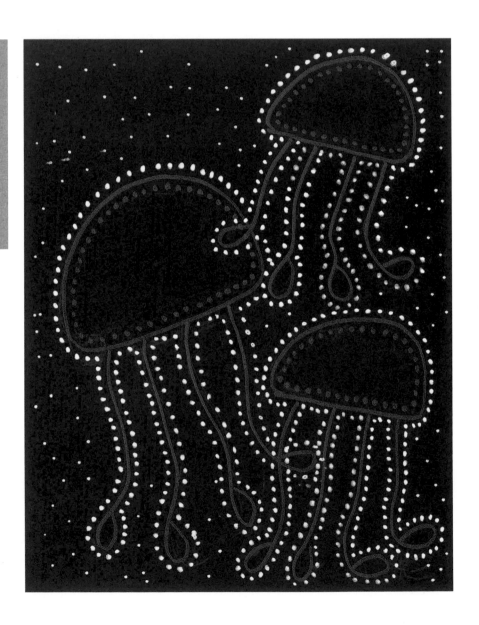

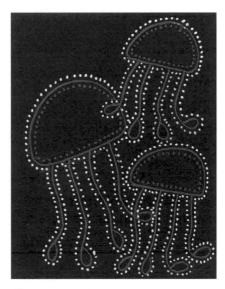

1. Draw three jellyfish bodies in pencil and trace with a gold or bronze metallic marker.

2. Draw dangling legs under each and trace with metallic marker. Add dots inside the body for definition.

3. Use white paint marker to add dots all around the jellyfish legs and body, as well as in the background.

ART SCHOOL 101: Aboriginal art is one of the oldest surviving art forms still practiced today. Many different styles exist, but dot paintings are probably the most famous. The technique can be done with tempera paint and cotton ear swabs, but you'll have a hard time getting the same result—this paint marker makes perfect dots with just one touch.

INDIAN HENNA HANDS

Project by Zach Stoller, owner of Thomas Elementary Art blog

Indian henna designs are ceremonial traditions that women of certain cultures use to adorn themselves. Zach Stoller likes to create projects that integrate academics and culture—like this one. Drawing these detailed patterns on paper with both thin and thick markers is a great way to study their amazing intricacy.

Project Checklist

- White paper, 12" x 18" (30.5 x 45.7 cm)
- Black fine point Sharpie marker
- Black ultra-fine point Sharpie marker
- Utility scissors
- Glue stick
- Two sheets of colored construction paper, 12" x 18" (30.5 x 45.7 cm)

ART SCHOOL 101: Henna has been around for a long time. It's even been found in ancient cave paintings in Sri Lanka. Made from a plant that grows in hot climates, the leaves, flowers, and twigs are ground into fine powder that contains natural dying properties called tannins. Hot water is then added to make a paste, and the mixture is applied to skin with a special cone-shaped tube.

1. 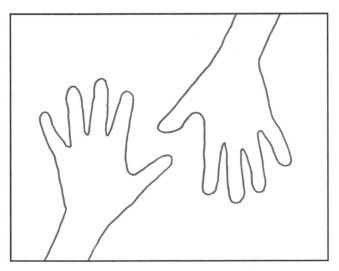 Trace your right and left hands on white paper.

2.  Draw shapes and lines inside the hands with a fine point marker.

3.  Draw henna designs with an ultra-fine point marker.

4.  Carefully cut out the hands and glue them to a sheet of construction paper. Cut around the hands, leaving an even edge all around, then glue to another sheet of construction paper.

NATIVE AMERICAN TOTEM PIZZA BOXES

Northwest Native Americans often included animal designs in their totem pole carvings. Drawing these faces on a pizza box with a large Sharpie marker is a great way to make your very own totem pole, one box at a time.

Project Checklist

- Pizza box
- Masking tape
- Pencil
- Black chisel tip Sharpie marker
- Crayons or colored pencils

The Raven

2. Use a ruler to draw center guidelines. Sketch shapes lightly with a pencil. See page 60 for a detailed drawing guide for the Raven.

1. Fold any box inside out so that any graphics are on the inside. Tape shut for a clean box canvas.

3. Trace all the art with the black chisel tip Sharpie marker. Fill in the black areas. Color in areas with crayons or colored pencils.

SOME OTHER SHAPES TO TRY:
The Sea Otter, the Dog, and the Bear. See the detailed drawing guides for each one on pages 61–63.

The Sea Otter   The Dog   The Bear

Draw the Raven

Native Americans believe that the Raven is a symbol of change and transformation.

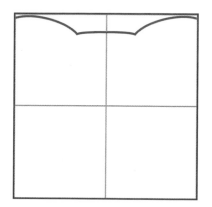

1. Draw the ears.

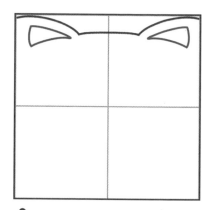

2. Add the inside ear shapes.

3. Add two curved eyebrows.

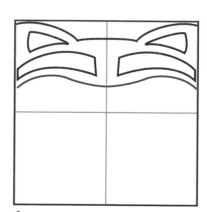

4. Draw a curvy brow line.

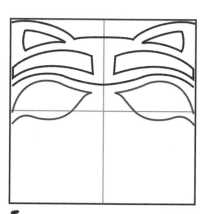

5. Add the outside eye shapes.

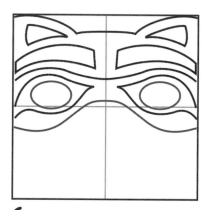

6. Draw circle eyes and a curvy nose line.

7. Draw the beak shape and inside mouth line.

8. Draw triangle and circle cheek shapes.

9. Fill in the solid areas.

Draw the Sea Otter

Native Americans believe Sea Otters are loyal and honest animals that bring humans luck.

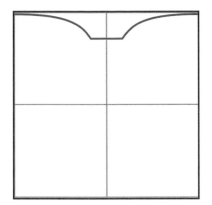

1. Draw the ears.

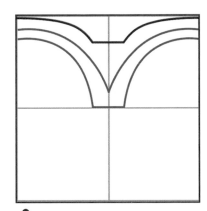

2. Add one connected eyebrow.

3. Draw two angled eyes.

4. Add the inside and outside eye lines.

5. Connect the eyes to the eyebrows with a line.

6. Draw the top of the nose.

7. Add the circles in the nose.

8. Add cheek lines.

9. Add the last cheek line, and fill in solid areas.

Draw the Dog

The Dog is believed to be a great ancestral spirit that helps people become strong and fierce, and is a symbol of all that is faithful.

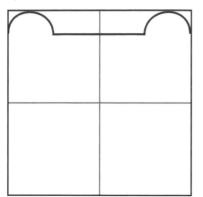

1. Draw the ears.

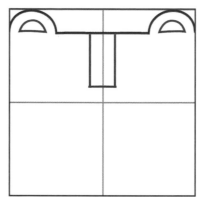

2. Add the inside ear and center nose line.

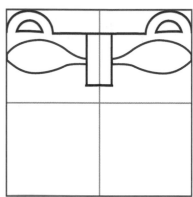

3. Draw the outer eye shapes.

4. Add the inner eye shapes

5. Draw two nose circles and an oval mouth.

6. Draw the outer mouth line.

7. Add teeth lines and two arms.

8. Draw a board shape behind the arms.

9. Add two legs and fill in all solid areas.

Draw the Bear

Native Americans believe the Bear spirit can help one perform great feats with skill and endurance.

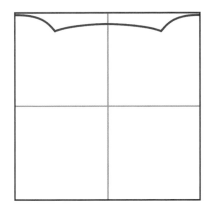

1. Draw the ears.

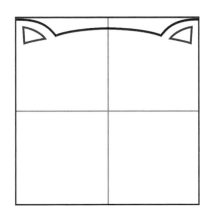

2. Add the inside ear shapes.

3. Draw two eyebrows.

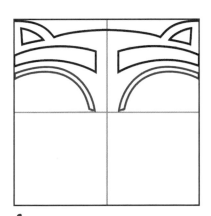

4. Add two curved lines.

5. Draw two circle eyes and outer lines.

6. Draw the nose.

7. Add sharp teeth lines.

8. Draw the outer mouth line and a tongue.

9. Add two arms and fill in all solid areas.

BLUE-AND-WHITE CHINA PLATE

Inexpensive ceramic plates and markers can make a pretty close imitation of this famous style of porcelain that originated in China. It's also an excellent way to practice drawing radial symmetry.

Project Checklist

- White plate *(ceramic, plastic, or paper)*
- Blue fine point Sharpie marker
- Blue brush tip Sharpie marker

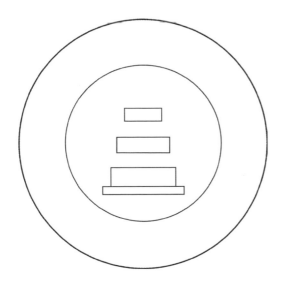

1. Using the fine point marker, draw a circle and start the building.

2. Add the side roof lines and building top.

3. Draw pole lines and curved roof lines.

4. Add landscaping around the building.

More on next page.

ART SCHOOL 101: Mass production of fine, translucent, blue-and-white porcelain started in the early 14th century at Jingdezhen, sometimes called the porcelain capital of China. The new ware was made possible by the export of cobalt from Persia, combined with the translucent white quality of Chinese porcelain. Cobalt blue was considered a precious commodity, with a value about twice that of gold.

5. Draw four petals and three rings.

6. Divide two thin rings with short lines. Add a dot in between each line.

7. Add radiating lines to the last ring.

8. Fill in the sky and outer ring with solid blue. The brush tip marker works best for this, as it leaves a smooth finish.

Safety Note: This plate is to be used for decoration only, as the marker will come off with even light handling. Consider it a benefit, though, as it allows for lots of "do overs" while drawing.

For Beginning Artists

Children who are just learning how to draw may still enjoy this project, but would fare better with fewer lines. Here is a substitute drawing that has a house with the same feel but a much simpler band going around the rim of the plate.

Plastic plates may be a good option for younger artists. They come in many cool shapes and look great with blue lines and color, just like the ceramic plates.

MEXICAN SUGAR SKULLS

Paper soup containers come with these great blank white sides. Here you can practice your symmetrical drawing in the round, and learn about the interesting history of Mexican sugar skulls.

Project Checklist

- Paper soup containers with matching lids
- Pencil
- Black fine point Sharpie marker
- Fine point Sharpie markers in assorted colors

1. Draw the design on the cup in pencil. Feel free to mix and match the motifs and decorations shown in these examples, but try to make the art symmetrical.

2. Trace the drawing with black marker.

3. Fill in the shapes with colored markers.

ART SCHOOL 101: Sugar skulls play a colorful role in Day of the Dead celebrations in Mexico, but making one in three-dimensional form can be tricky and, at the very least, time consuming. These white soup containers work perfectly, as they're ready to go and have the basic shape of a head built right in.

AFRICAN LION

Here's a simple way to draw an impressive lion with a giant built-in mane. Use the transparent quality of coffee filters to help make your drawing as symmetrical as possible.

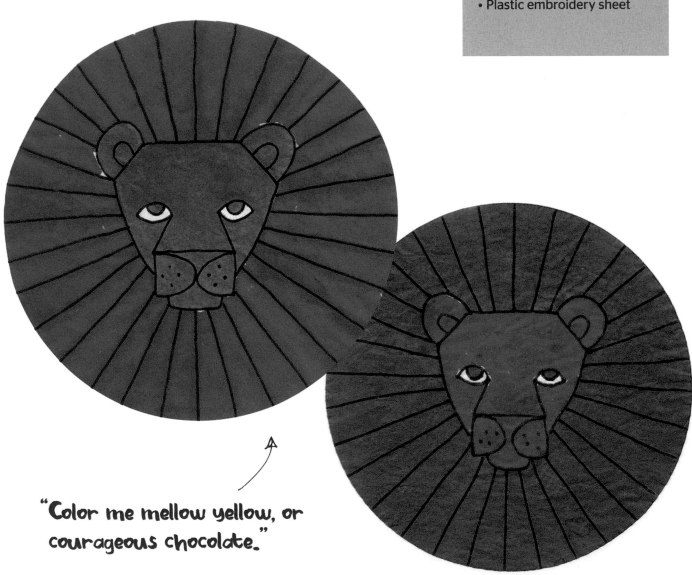

"Color me mellow yellow, or courageous chocolate."

 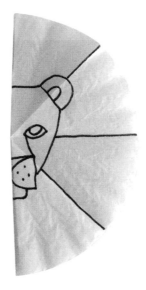 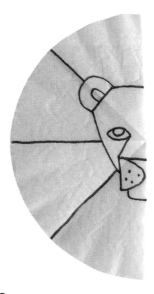

1. Use a steam iron to flatten the filters to round circles. Fold in half three times so that you have a cone shape as shown. Crease the edges with your fingertips.

2. Open the filter to see a half circle. Draw half of the face as shown with a pencil and trace with a marker. Trace the three creased lines as shown.

3. Flip the filter over and you will see the lines. Trace to the other side with a marker.

4. Open the filter and add more mane lines in between the ones already there.

5. Place the filter on a plastic embroidery sheet and paint with the liquid watercolor paint. Let dry. Some of the mesh lines will transfer onto the filter. When dry, a quick press with a steam iron again will make the filter look crisp and flat.

Just say no to boring notebooks!

You can color me happy.

ROCK STAR PENGUINS

Painting on rocks is fun and easy for kids when they're working with a firm marker instead of a soft paintbrush. And the high-contrast color scheme couldn't get any simpler than with these little black-and-white penguins made with decorative black rocks—typically used for flower arranging—from your local craft store.

Project Checklist

- Decorative black rocks or stones, matte surface (*found at craft stores and online*)
- Sharpie oil-based paint markers in black, orange, and white
- Spray sealer

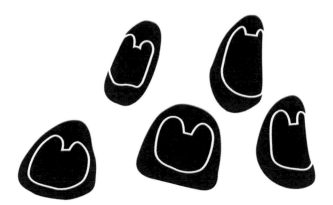

1. Use the white marker to draw the outline on each rock as shown.

2. Fill in the area with the white marker. Let dry until the surface is no longer sticky.

3. Draw a triangle beak in orange.

4. Add two eyes in black. To keep the paint from rubbing off, seal the rocks with a coat of spray sealer. Let dry.

SNAIL MAIL ANIMAL ENVELOPES

Here are six animal faces, in very simple form, that turn a boring brown envelope into a work of art. Each has space in the middle to add the address of a lucky recipient.

Project Checklist
- Envelopes, brown kraft paper type
- Black fine point Sharpie marker
- Black ultra-fine point Sharpie marker
- White water-based Sharpie paint marker

Plenty of room for the address!

Beaver

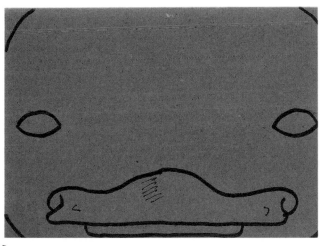 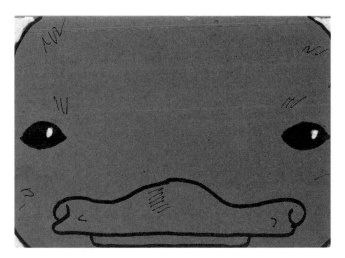

Duck

1. Start with a brown envelope.

2. Draw the face with a fine point marker, then add details with an ultra-fine point marker.

3. Fill in black eyes and the white background.

4. Add highlights to each eye for a final touch.

More on next page.

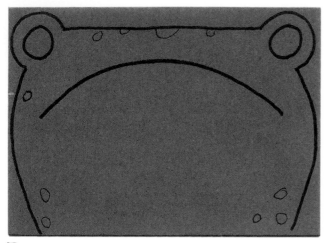 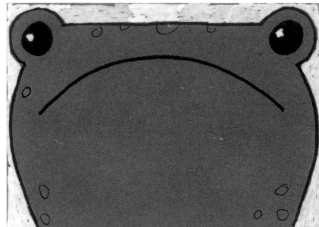

Frog

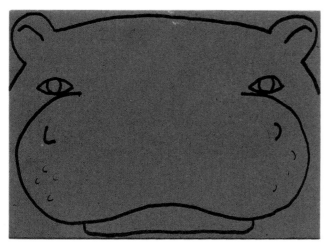 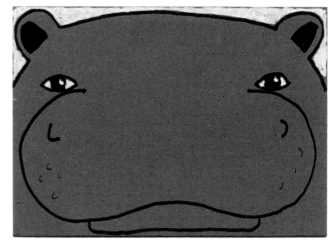

Hippo

Sheep

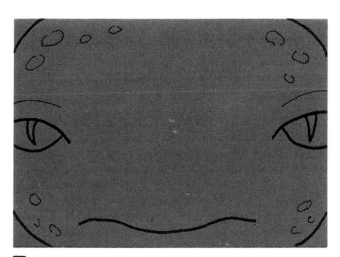

Turtle

CITYSCAPE DUCT TAPE NOTEBOOK

Add a fun cover to your composition notebook with a little duct tape and Sharpie paint markers. The opaque quality of the paint markers contrasts nicely with the shiny tape.

Project Checklist

- Composition notebook
- Black duct tape
- Utility scissors
- Sharpie water-based paint markers in assorted colors

1. Start with an inexpensive composition book.

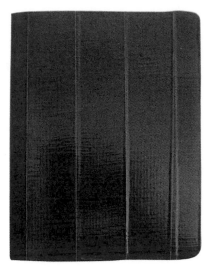

2. Use utility scissors to cut strips of duct tape and apply vertically to the book cover, overlapping slightly. Wrap the ends over the edges.

3. Draw the outline of city buildings with paint markers. The ridges of the tape will help you draw straight lines. Add a moon and window details to the buildings.

ART SCHOOL 101:

If paint markers are not in your budget, create a cityscape or other drawing using the metallic silver variety. They look great on the black duct tape background.

CONCENTRIC CIRCLES T-SHIRT

Project by Ana Dziengel, owner of Babble Dabble Do website

Art and design mom blogger Ana Dziengel uses an embroidery hoop to help keep the swirling Sharpie marker color within a neat and tidy frame.

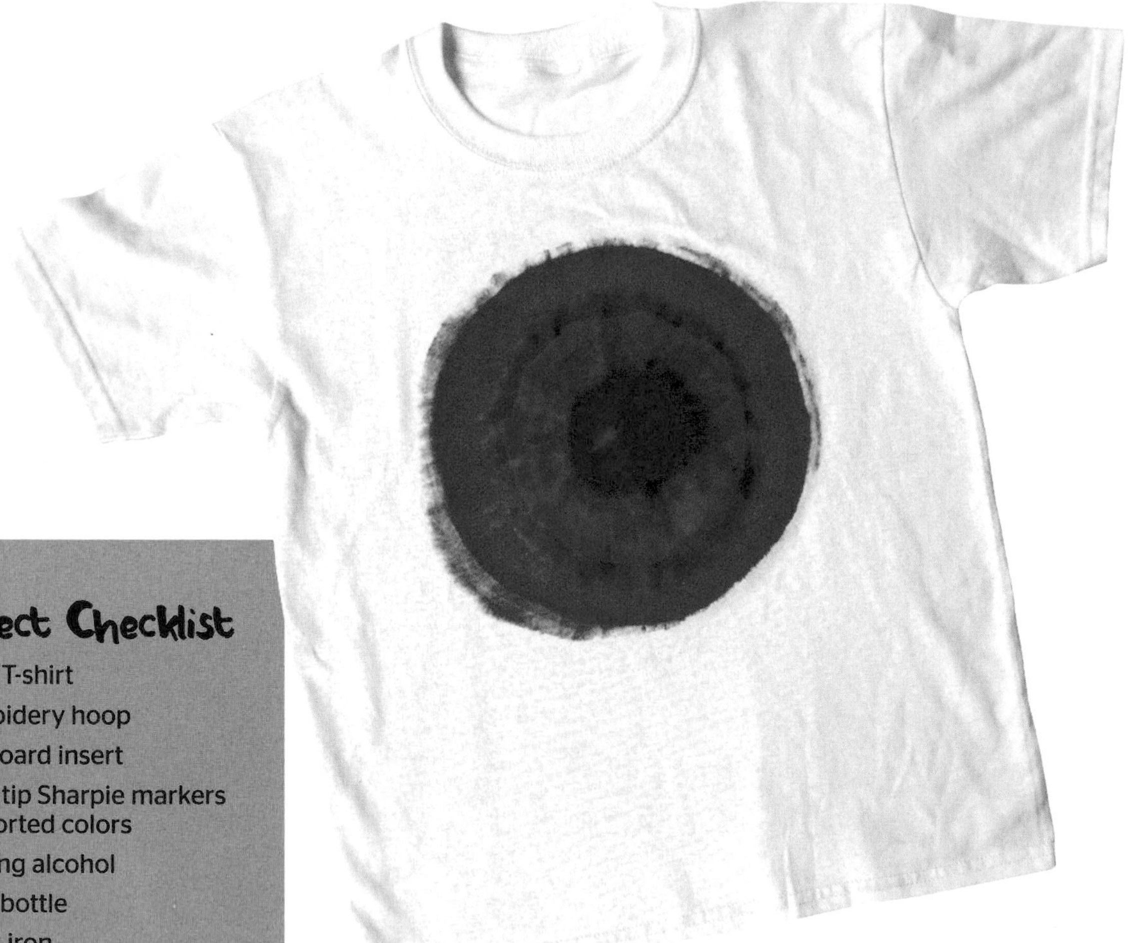

Project Checklist

- White T-shirt
- Embroidery hoop
- Cardboard insert
- Brush tip Sharpie markers in assorted colors
- Rubbing alcohol
- Spray bottle
- Steam iron

1. Choose an embroidery hoop that's the right size for your shirt. I used a 9" (22.9 cm) hoop on an adult size small T-shirt.

2. Place the hoop rings on the shirt, centered in the middle. Insert the cardboard between the layers of fabric so the marker won't bleed through. Color a small circle in the center of the hoop.

3. Continue coloring rings around the circle until the hoop is full. The more marker that's applied, the darker the results.

4. Pour rubbing alcohol into a spray bottle and saturate the colored fabric. (If you're lucky, your local drug store may sell rubbing alcohol in a spray container.) Let the shirt dry for 30 minutes before removing the hoops. Set the color with a hot iron and hand wash in cold water before wearing.

OP ART SOCCER BALL

A soccer ball turns into a work of op art with the help of some careful coloring. The built-in hexagon shapes can change into cubes when they're split into three shapes as shown.

Project Checklist

- White soccer ball
- Brush tip Sharpie markers in assorted colors
- Water-based sealer (*such as Mod Podge aerosol spray*)

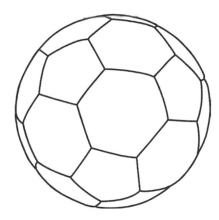

1. Start with a clean white soccer ball. If you can't find one in a sporting goods store, many are available online.

2. Look for the five-sided pentagon shapes and color them with your darkest marker color. They sometimes have logos that need to be covered over and will look better when colored in.

3. Starting with one of the hexagons, draw a diamond shape as shown and fill in.

4. Choose a color that contrasts with the first color and draw another diamond shape as shown and fill in.

5. Choose another color that contrasts with the first two and finish the hexagon shape as shown.

6. Continue filling in the remaining hexagons with the diamond shapes so they look like cubes. Try to keep dark colors separated by light colors so all the sides show up well. Spray the ball with a sealer.

FLOWER POWER MUG

A coffee mug with your own drawing on it makes for a special gift. This simple flower filled with bright marker color is super easy, and perfect for little hands to do.

Project Checklist

- Ceramic coffee mug *(from craft store or dollar store)*
- Black fine point Sharpie marker
- Brush tip Sharpie markers in assorted colors
- Oven
- Dishwasher-safe, water-based sealer *(such as Dishwasher-Safe Mod Podge)*

1. Draw a zigzag grass line all around the bottom of the cup with fine point marker.

2. Draw a stem and flower center.

3. Add flower petals attached to the center.

4. Add leaves to the stem and draw pins between each flower petal.

5. Carefully fill the flower with brush tip markers. Try to avoid bumping into the black line as the colors will smear.

6. Place the mug in a cold oven. Turn the temperature to 350°F (about 175°C) and bake for 30 minutes. Allow to cool in oven. If the colors fade more than desired, add color and bake again for the same amount of time. Apply dishwasher-safe, water-based sealer to the outside of the cup. Apply two to three coats. Let cure for 28 days and then hand wash only for best results.

Safety Note

When decorating your mug, be sure to avoid decorating any surfaces that could come in contact with food, drink, or your mouth.

CORK COASTERS

If you decorate a cork coaster with wood grain–looking lines and fill them with bright colors, you can easily create a pretty, organic design.

Project Checklist

- Cork coasters
- Black fine point Sharpie markers
- Colored fine point Sharpie markers
- Water-based sealer (*such as Mod Podge aerosol spray*)

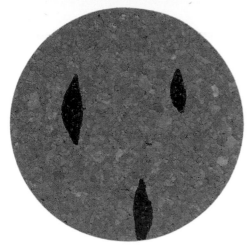

1. Draw three eye shapes with a black marker on the coaster. Be sure to leave space between them.

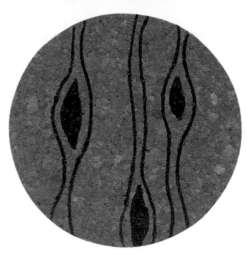

2. Draw wavy lines on both sides of the eye shapes. Pretend the lines are like water, flowing around the eye shape.

3. Fill in the remaining space with more wavy lines. The lines may attach to others if space is tight. The goal is to not have any lines cross over each other.

4. Fill in each line with a different color. When complete, spray with sealer.

ART SCHOOL 101: Try limiting the marker bands of color to just four or so. This will mean that each color needs to be repeated a few times. The repeating color will create a more harmonious finish.

Your next project could come from the recycling bin.

AROUND THE HOUSE

CD TERRARIUM

Recycle an old CD case by decorating it with a fun drawing on the front, then growing grass inside. It's a great way to mix a little science into your art, while keeping a few more CD cases out of our landfills.

Project Checklist

- CD case (*the ¼"-thick type*)
- Oil-based Sharpie paint markers in assorted colors
- Potting soil
- Grass seed
- Rubber band

1. Remove the insert from a CD case. It pops out when gently pried apart.

2. Draw flowers on one side with paint markers. Include the root system in white.

3. Dampen a small amount of potting soil and pack into the open bottom of the CD case. Sprinkle grass seed on top. Close and wrap with a rubber band to keep the case from opening up. Stand in indirect sunlight for about one week and see what grows!

ART SCHOOL 101: Many students start learning about plant systems as early as kindergarten. Adding roots to this flower drawing turns an art project into a science one as well.

RECYCLED TiN CAN PENCiL HOLDER

Here's an easy way to make an old tin can look cool and graphic. Give it a new surface by wrapping it in metal tape and adding lots of marker lines and patterns.

Project Checklist

- Empty tin can *(such as those used for soup or sauce)*
- Black fine point Sharpie marker
- Metal tape *(found at local hardware stores)*
- Utility scissors

1. Clean the can and remove the paper wrapper.

2. Cut a strip of tape that is a little longer than the circumference of the can. Apply the tape to the can by slowly removing the paper as shown.

3. Add another strip of tape around the bottom of the can, and then finally one around the middle.

4. Use the built-in ridges in the can as a guide to draw marker lines. Continue with patterns and fill in as desired.

Variations

Simplify. Focus on making nice bands of color. Brush tip markers work best for this.

Mix It Up. Keep the black and silver foil look, and add color just in the middle.

ART SCHOOL 101: Many soup cans have a lining that keeps them from being easily recycled. Do our landfills a favor and turn them into beautiful and useful containers instead.

CARDBOARD HOUSE

Save old, clean corrugated cardboard boxes and turn them into a lesson on how to make a three-dimensional form from geometric shapes. Thick and thin black markers are all you need to add some interesting architectural details to your buildings.

Project Checklist

- Old, clean corrugated cardboard
- Paper cutter
- House drawing templates *(see pages 113–119)*
- Black fine point Sharpie marker
- Black ultra-fine point Sharpie marker
- Masking tape
- Craft glue

DIMENSIONS OF OUR HOUSE:

- Peaked sides: 6" (15.2 cm) wide 10" (25.4 cm) high
- Plain sides: 5" (12.7 cm) wide 7" (17.8 cm) high
- Roof pieces: 6¼" (15.9 cm) wide 5" (12.7 cm) high

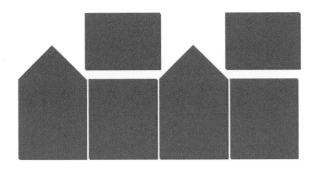

1. Cut two squares or rectangles from cardboard, and then two peaked house ends. Lastly, cut two roof rectangles that are a little wider than the house. (See opposite for the dimensions of our house.) A good old-fashioned paper cutter works best.

2. Using the drawing templates as guides, draw the main features of the house with a fine point marker as shown.

3. Add fine details with an ultra-fine point marker. Tape the four house sides together from the inside with masking tape. Tape the two roof panels together along the long side. Run a small line of glue along the top edge of the standing house, then gently place the roof on top and let dry.

ART SCHOOL 101: Children love to make three-dimensional things, and this project can stir all kinds of imaginative play and creative thinking. Houses can lead to villages and cities, and maybe even inspire some future architects.

DOODLE LIGHT SWITCHES

You can get the look of drawing on your wall by keeping it on your room's light switch. Those smooth plates make great canvases that can show off all your amazing art.

Project Checklist

- Drawing templates *(see pages 121 and 123)*
- Light switch plates *(found at hardware stores)*
- Scrap paper
- Pencil
- Black fine point Sharpie marker
- Brush tip Sharpie markers in assorted colors

Doodle Bugs

Flower Garden

House on a Hill

Friendly Monster

1. Using the drawing templates as guides, use a pencil to draw the design on the switch plates. Pencil lines don't show very well on the plastic, so make a practice drawing on paper first.

2. Use the fine point marker and start with the black outline shapes of your drawing. Be careful not to touch the marker, as it needs a few seconds to dry.

3. Fill in the shapes with the brush tip markers. They make a smooth finish, but will start to blend with the black if you bump into it.

HAND-COLORED TRIVET

Sharpie brush tip markers are the perfect tool for neatly coloring in all the little curvy shapes in this abstract pattern.

Project Checklist

- Ceramic tile
- Pencil
- Brush tip Sharpie markers in assorted colors
- Water-based sealer (*such as Mod Podge aerosol spray*)

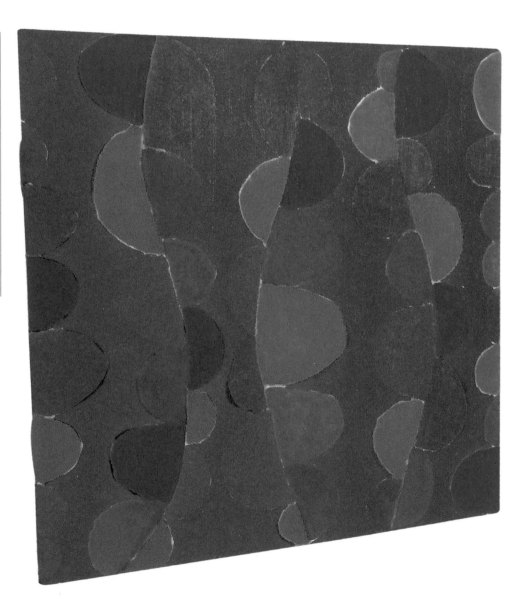

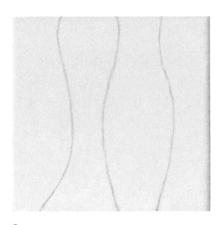

1. Draw three wavy lines in pencil on a ceramic tile.

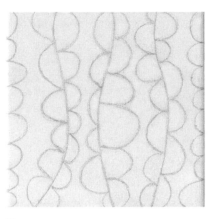

2. Draw half circles attached to each line as shown. Make some large and some small, taking care to not have any ends match up.

3. Color in the half circles with marker. Change the colors so they do not match up across the wavy line. If they do match up, the center wavy line will not show up as clearly.

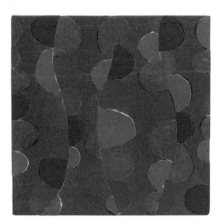

4. Fill in the background with one color. Apply the water-based sealer to the surface. Let dry and apply extra coats as desired.

For Younger Artists

This easier variation, which uses fewer lines, features a warm-cool palette.

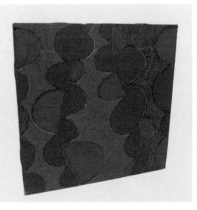

GIRAFFE FINGER PUPPETS

For a little bit of puppet fun, use the yellow color of rubber gloves to make a family of cute giraffes.

Have a puppet show with your new friends.

1. Cut a finger from the rubber glove with scissors.

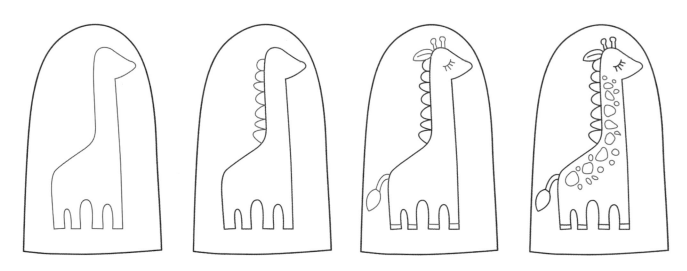

2. Draw the giraffe with an ultra-fine point black marker, and fill spots with brown. Color the background with blue and green.

KIDS' ART GALLERY

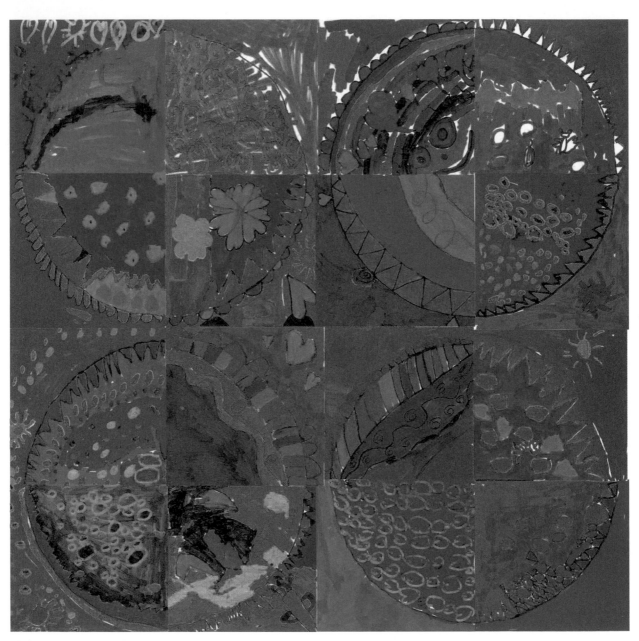

Quarter Circle
Group project by Ms. Boccalatte's 1st grade class

Mighty Oak
Leaf drawing by Olivia R., age 5

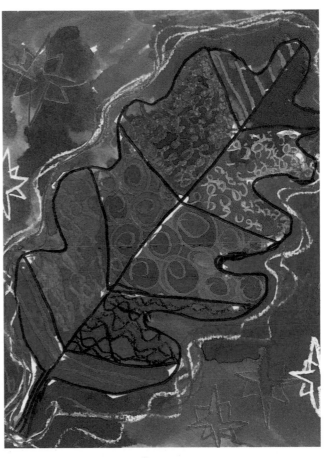

Shimmering Leaf
Watercolor and marker drawing by Sara G., age 7

Fancy Fish
Paint marker on cardboard by Astrid S., age 5

Nutcracker
Tempera painting with gold marker by Aidan G., age 7

Tiki Drawing
by Nola L., age 8

Cartoon Hero
by Aiden S., age 9

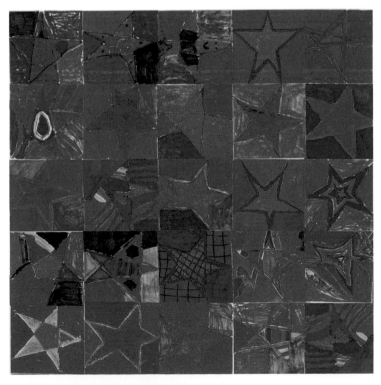

Star Paper Quilt
Group project by Ms. Bayless's 2nd grade class

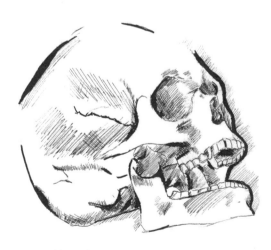

Skull Sketch
by Emil S., age 9

TEMPLATES

Tooled Metal Bug
See project on pages 36–37

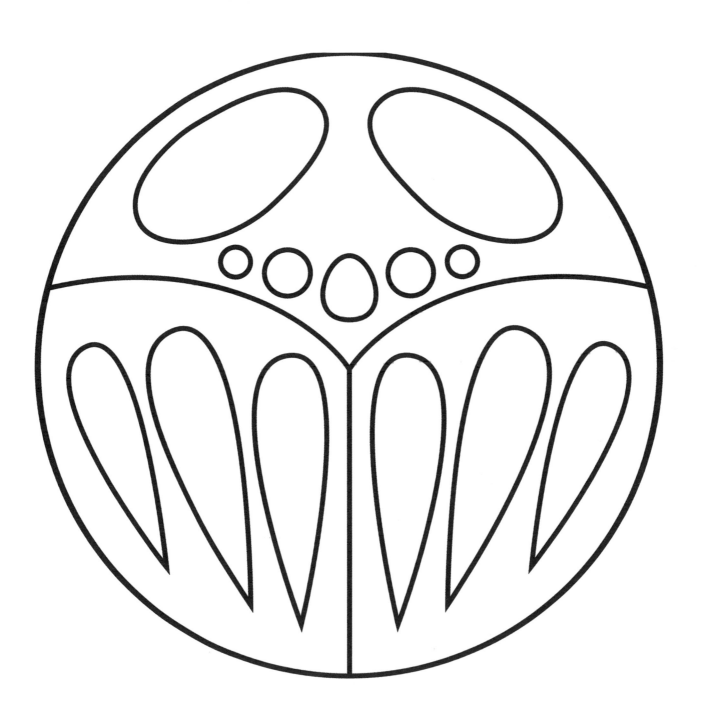

African Mask Drawings
See project on pages 52–53

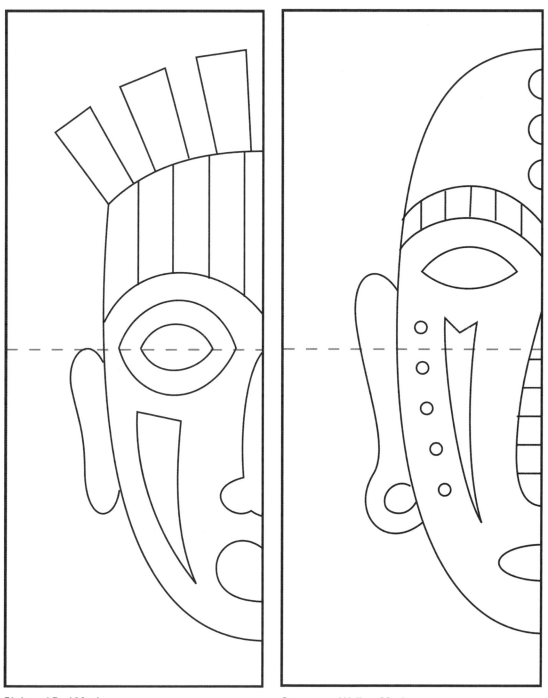

Pink and Red Mask

Orange and Yellow Mask

Cardboard House (Front)
See project on pages 96–97

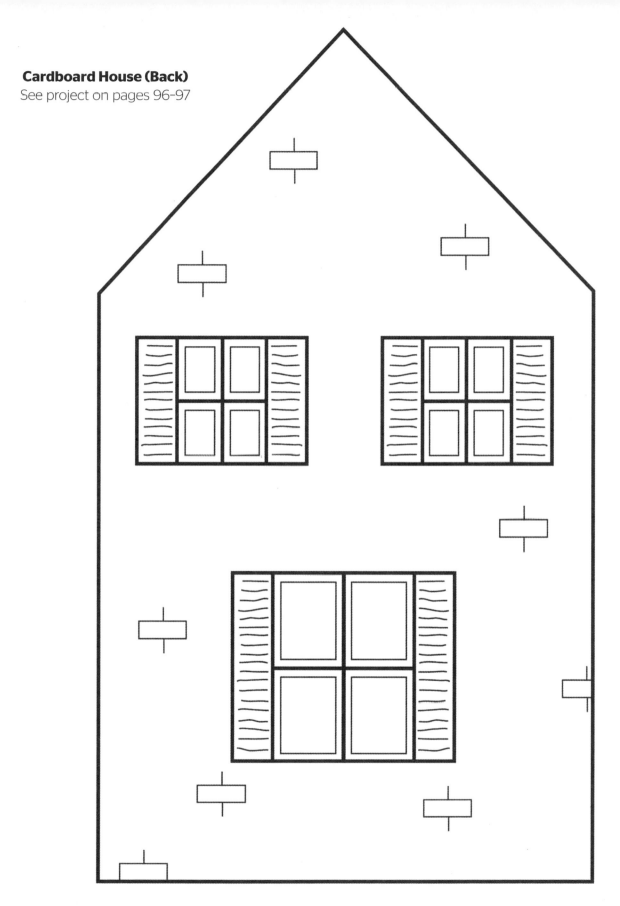

Cardboard House (Back)
See project on pages 96–97

Cardboard House (Sides)
See project on pages 96–97

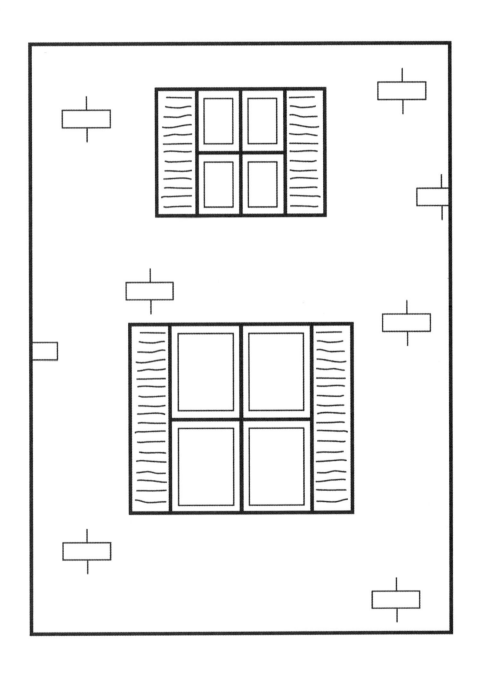

Cardboard House (Roof)
See project on pages 96–97

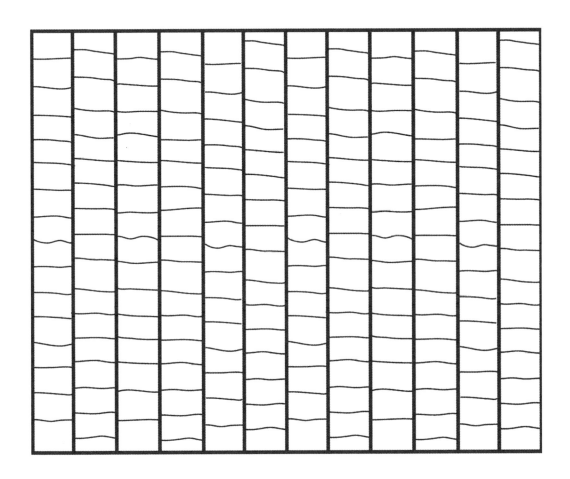

Doodle Light Switches
See project on pages 98–99

Doodle Bugs

Flower Garden

Doodle Light Switches
See project on pages 98–99

House on a Hill

Friendly Monster

CONTRIBUTORS

Gail Bartel
That Artist Woman blog
thatartistwoman.org
Project: Shimmering Sea Life
Pages: 46-47
Gail Bartel has been an art educator for the last 13 years, teaching kids from kindergarten to middle school. She has blogged for the last 7 years at That Artist Woman, and her favorite mediums are paint, papier-mâché, clay, and batik. When she isn't teaching, you can find her in her studio designing new projects and painting up a storm.

Mary Beggs Bosley
MaryMaking blog
marymaking.blogspot.com
Project: Picasso Tissue Paper Portrait
Pages: 34-35
Mary Beggs Bosley has been blogging and teaching private children's art classes to kindergarteners through sixth graders for the past 6 years. Her background in graphic design and fine art allows for inspiration from unexpected materials, and when combined with the traditional, makes for fun mixed-media projects.

Ana Dziengel
Babble Dabble Do website
babbledabbledo.com
Project: Concentric Circles T-Shirt
Pages: 82-83
In 2012, Ana Dziengel left behind an architecture career to be a stay-at-home-mom, professional crafter, amateur scientist, and impromptu art teacher to her three children. She blogs about kids art, design, science, and engineering, and is a regular contributor to PBS Parents Crafts for Kids. Her YouTube series *Creative Basics* explores art and science projects and play recipes that anyone who knows a child should have in their toolkit.

Nic Hahn
Mini Matisse blog
MiniMatisse.blogspot.com
Project: Tooled Metal Bug
Pages: 36-37
Nic Hahn has spent her career teaching art to preschool students through adults. She enjoys breaking down the creative process so that all learners may feel success in art. Nic celebrates and shares her classroom happenings on her blog.

Laura Lohmann
Painted Paper Art blog
paintedpapeart.com
Project: Folk Art Landscape
Pages: 48-49
Laura Lohmann has been teaching elementary art for nearly 20 years in Ohio. She enjoys seeing her students start with a blank canvas and explore various art materials to create beautiful masterpieces. She also loves creating fun, colorful projects from painted paper made in her art room.

Zach Stoller
Thomas Elementary Art blog
thomaselementaryart.blogspot.com
Project: Indian Henna Hands
Pages: 56-57
Zach Stoller is an elementary art teacher in Dublin, Ohio. He has been teaching since 2006 and blogging since 2009. His lessons often integrate a wide range of sources, including both cultural and academic areas. Students in his classroom focus on creativity while simultaneously learning new art-making techniques and furthering their artistic education.

Cheryl Trowbridge
Teach Kids Art website
teachkidsart.net
Project: Warm and Cool Echo Flowers
Pages: 32-33
Cheryl Trowbridge has been teaching art to kids of all ages for more than 20 years. She is the founder of Teach Kids Art, a website dedicated to helping parents and teachers share the joy of art with the kids in their lives.

ADDITIONAL RESOURCES

Suggested Reading

Gina Capaldi, *Native Americans: Customs, Costumes, Legends and Lore* Good Apple, 1997

School of Arts Magazine www.davisart.com

Arts & Activities Magazine www.artsandactivities.com

Recommended Websites

Adventures of an Art Teacher KatieMorrisArt.com

Art Bar Blog ArtBarBlog.com

Art Ed Guru ArtEdGuru.com

Art for Small Hands ArtForSmallHands.com

Art with Mr. E ArtWithMrE.com

Art with Mrs. Nguyen www.ArtWithMrsNguyen.com

Art Teachers Hate Glitter athglitter.com

California Arts Council cac.ca.gov

Cassie Stephens CassieStephens.blogspot.com

ClipArt ETC etc.usf.edu/clipart

Creative Corner CreativeCornerNY.blogspot.com

Deep Space Sparkle DeepSpaceSparkle.com

Dryden Art DrydenArt.weebly.com

iPad Art Room iPadArtRoom.com

John Post JohnPost.us

Mrs. Knight's Smartest Artists DolvinArtKnight.blogspot.com

National Art Education Association arteducators.org

No Corner Suns NoCornerSuns.blogspot.com

Organized Chaos MsNovak.blogspot.com

Polka Dot Spot ArtPolkaDotSpot.blogspot.com.au

Sharpie Creations Gallery www.sharpie.com/en-US/creations

Smart Class ElementaryArtFun.blogspot.com

The Art Curator for Kids ArtCuratorForKids.com

The Art of Education TheArtOfEd.com

The Artful Parent ArtfulParent.com

There's a Dragon in My Art Room plbrown.blogspot.com

Thoughts on Arting PurteeArt1.weebly.com

Tinkerlab tinkerlab.com

ACKNOWLEDGMENTS

I'd like to begin by thanking all the creative bloggers who generously contributed to this book. I know you have very busy lives, probably working online only after your daytime jobs and parenting work is done. You all were so helpful in sharing what you do best, and I truly am grateful for every extra bit of creativity you added to this book.

I also would like to thank the students, teachers, and parents at Dixie Canyon Community Charter in Sherman Oaks, California, for your unwavering support of the arts. Every year the PTA spends countless fundraiser hours making sure that students at Dixie have access to visual and performing art classes. You are my heroes. (I'd also like give a shout-out to Mila for her monster drawing that inspired my light switch project. It was so perfect that I merely did my best to copy it.)

And finally, to my husband and son, Steve and Matthew, who pretty much gave up the kitchen table and many hot meals while I created this book. Your belief that my hard work would one day pay off helped me more than you know, and I love you for it.

ABOUT THE AUTHOR

 Kathy Barbro is an art teacher and blogger whose art career began at the Minneapolis College of Art & Design. After years of graphic design work, she found her passion in working with children when her son's school was found to have no art instruction or teacher. Teaching led to blogging, where she has shared hundreds of projects over the past ten years through her site, artprojectsforkids.org. This is her first book.

INDEX